For My Children

FOR MY CHILDREN

The Teachings of Her Holiness
Sri Mata Amritanandamayi Devi

Mata Amritanandamayi Mission Trust
Amritapuri, Kerala

For My Children
Translated from the original Malayalam *Amrita Mozhikal* into English by Swami Ramakrishnananda Puri

Published by:
  Mata Amritanandamayi Mission Trust
  Amritapuri P.O., Kollam Dt.,
  Kerala 690525, INDIA
  Website: www.amritapuri.org
  Email: info@theammashop.org

First edition 1986	3,000 Copies
Second - fifteenth edition	36,000 copies
Sixteenth edition 2012	2,000 copies

Contents

Foreword

The essence of India lies in her culture, the ultimate aim of which is Self-realization for everyone—to raise the ordinary person to the heights of supreme consciousness. While India turns to the West for material comforts and pleasures, the West, disillusioned with the hollow grandeur of materialism, is increasingly turning to the perennial philosophies of the East for guidance and refuge. From ancient times to the present day, enlightened mahatmas [great souls] have been born in India, with the purpose of leading seekers of the ultimate Truth to their goal.

"Why would I need a spiritual guide?" we may ask. "After reading a few books, can't I simply make my own way along the spiritual path?" A person who wishes to become a doctor has to study with learned professors. Even after graduating from medical school, he or she will have to work as an intern at a hospital under the guidance of experienced doctors. Many years will be spent to fulfil the dream of becoming a doctor. What, then, can be said about the aspiration to realize the supreme Truth? If you want spiritual wisdom, you have to seek out an authentic spiritual master who has studied, practiced and experienced the Truth—who has become a living embodiment of Truth itself.

What distinguishes a true teacher from an impostor? In the presence of the enlightened sage, who is immersed in divinity, one feels a tangible, unmistakable aura of love and tranquillity. One observes how he or she treats everyone equally, with a love that is boundless and completely unconditional, regardless of that person's virtues or vices, social position, wealth, race or religion. Every word and action of a true master serves to uplift us spiritually. In him or her there will be no trace of ego or selfishness. The *mahatma* receives and serves one and all with open arms.

An ideal example of such a master is Sri Mata Amritanandamayi Devi, who is revered throughout the world as an embodiment of the Universal

Mother. This book contains selections from her spiritual teachings, and answers many frequently asked questions. Mother's words have the simplicity of a village girl, and, at the same time, the profound and immediate quality of someone speaking directly from divine experience. Her teachings are universal and applicable to our daily lives, whether we are serious spiritual aspirants, mildly interested seekers, or even sceptics.

Mother's teachings demand that we think. These are not flowery utterances that spoon-feed the mind and intellect. On the contrary, we have to use our intellect and intuition to contemplate Her words in order to bring out their full, implied meaning. At times it may seem that some idea expressed in this little book is incomplete or not thoroughly explained. When Mother was consulted or further elaboration, she said, "Let them think it over." That is to say, the principles that are expounded require contemplation, rather than excessive explanations. If you are serious about Self-realization and you dedicate yourself sincerely and with humility to the study and practice of these teachings, you can certainly reach the goal. Open this book at a random page and see if Mother's words don't speak to you.

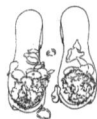

A Brief Sketch of Mother's Life

"From the moment I was born I had an intense love for the Name of God, so much so that I would repeat the Name incessantly with every breath. In this way, there was a constant flow of divine thoughts in my mind, irrespective of where I was or what I was doing. This unbroken recollection of God, with love and devotion, would be of immense help to any aspirant in attaining divine realization."

Born on September 27, 1953, in a remote fishing village on the southwest coast of India, Sudhamani [Pure Gem], as her parents named her, bore signs of divinity right from the start. She was born with an unusual dark blue complexion. She started speaking her mother tongue, Malayalam, when she was barely six months old, and also started walking at this age, without first having gone through a crawling stage as babies normally do.

At the age of five, Sudhamani was composing

devotional songs to Sri Krishna, songs that were filled with love and deep longing for the Divine. The verses, though childlike in their innocent simplicity, were filled with extraordinary philosophical and mystical depth. She became known throughout the village for her songs and her beautiful, soulful voice. When she was only nine years old she had to leave school because her mother fell ill with rheumatism and could no longer attend to the housework. Getting up long before dawn and working until eleven at night, Sudhamani cooked for the entire family, tended the cows, goats and ducks, washed all the family's clothes, cleaned the house and the yard, and so on. Whatever time she could spare during her long workdays was spent in meditation and in heartfelt song and prayers to Lord Krishna.

Before long, she was having many divine visions and experienced the state of *samadhi* [oneness with God]. By the time she was seventeen, this state had deepened into permanent union with the Divine. She experienced the world as a manifestation of the all-pervading One. The mere mention of God would plunge her mind into deep inner absorption.

At this time, following a vision, a strong desire took hold of her to realize the Divine Mother. Forsaking rest, food and shelter, Sudhamani underwent severe austerities. This period of intense *tapas* [austerities] culminated in the appearance of the Divine Mother before her as an effulgence of Divine Light that merged with her. After this, Sudhamani felt no inclination to mix with people, and spent most of her time in solitude, enjoying the bliss of Self-realization.

One day she heard a voice within her say: "My child, I dwell in the hearts of all beings and have no fixed abode. You have not come to this world merely to enjoy the unalloyed bliss of the Self, but to comfort suffering humanity. From now on, worship Me in the hearts of all beings by relieving them of the suffering of worldly existence."

Since that day, Sudhamani, whom everyone began to call "Amma" [Mother], has devoted every moment of her life to the welfare of humanity. Every day thousands of people flock to Her from all over the world to receive her love, her guidance and her blessings, and to simply experience her presence. Mother has also established a vast network of charitable, spiritual and educational activities, which include hospitals for the poor, orphanages, houses the homeless, an old-age home, a regular pension for tens of thousands of women among the poorest of the poor, free meals and disaster relief. These practical manifestations of Mother's compassion continue to grow and expand at a tremendous rate. Her organization, M.A. Math, has been made an NGO by the United Nations.

Mother listens patiently to all who come to her as they tell her about their problems. She comforts them as only a loving mother can do, yet even more so, and alleviates their suffering. She says: "Different types of people come to see Mother, some out of devotion, others for a solution to their worldly problems or to be cured of their diseases. Mother discards no one. How could she reject anyone? Is anyone different from Mother? Are we not all beads strung on the one life thread? Each person sees Mother according to his or her level of understanding. Both those who love me and those who hate me are the same to me."

About Mother

1.   My children, the mother who gave birth to you may look after matters relating to this life. Nowadays, even this is rare. But Mother's aim is to lead you in such a way that you will enjoy bliss in all your future lives.

2.   It can be painful when the pus in a wound is squeezed out. But would a sincere doctor refrain from doing this just because it hurts? Similarly, when your *vasanas* [innate tendencies] are being removed, you will experience some pain. This is for your own good. Just as a gardener removes the pests that destroy a sprouting plant, Mother is removing your negative tendencies.

3.   It may be easy for you to love Mother, but that is not enough. Try to see Mother in everyone. My children, do not think that Mother is confined to this body alone.

4.   My children, to truly love Mother is to love all beings in the world equally.

5.   The love of those who love Mother only when Mother shows them love is not real love. Only those who cling to Mother's feet in spite of her scoldings have true devotion.

6.   Those who live in this ashram and learn from Mother's every action will become liberated. If Mother's words and deeds are contemplated, you need not study a single scripture.

7.   The mind has to hold on to something, but this is not possible without faith. When a seed is sown, its upward growth depends on the root going deep into the soil. Without being rooted in faith, spiritual growth is not possible.

8.   No matter where you are, you should either silently chant your mantra or meditate. If this isn't possible, you can read spiritual books. Don't waste time. Even if a million rupees are lost Mother won't

feel as much concern as she feels when a single moment of yours is wasted. Money can be regained, but lost time can never be regained. My children, be always aware of the value of time.

9.   My children, Mother does not say that you should believe in Mother or in a God in heaven. It is enough to believe in yourself. Everything is within you.

10.   If you really love Mother, do spiritual practice and know the Self. Mother loves you without expecting anything from you. It would be enough for Mother if she could see her children enjoying eternal peace, oblivious of night and day.

11.   Only when you selflessly love even an ant will Mother consider that you truly love her. Mother doesn't consider any other kind of love as real love. So-called love that is born out of selfishness makes Mother feel as if she's burning.

12.   Mother's nature varies according to your

thoughts and actions. The form of the Lord as Narasimha [the divine man-lion], who roared and pounced with such great ferocity on the demon king Hiranyakashipu, was peaceful in Prahlada's presence. God, who is pure and beyond all attributes adopted different moods according to their actions. Similarly, Mother's behaviour changes according to the attitudes of her children. Mother, whom you praise as Snehamayi [the embodiment of love], may at times appear to be Krooramayi [the cruel one]. This is to correct the flaws found in her children's behaviour. Mother's only intention is to make you good.

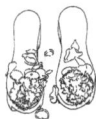

The Spiritual Master

13. Once you know of a particular shop where you can purchase everything you need, why wander among all the other shops in the market? That would be useless and a waste of time. Similarly, once you have found a perfect master, there is no need for you to wander; just do your spiritual practice and strive to reach the goal.

14. A spiritual master is indispensable for a seeker. If a toddler goes near the edge of a pond, the mother will point out the danger and lead the child away. In the same way, the master will give the disciple whatever instructions are necessary. The master's attention will always be on the disciple.

15. Although God is all-pervasive, the presence of a spiritual master is unique. The wind blows everywhere, but we enjoy a special coolness in the shade of a tree. Doesn't the breeze that blows through the leaves of a tree have a soothing effect on those

who are travelling in the hot sun? In the same way, a spiritual master is necessary for those who live in the scorching heat of worldly existence. The master's presence gives us inner peace and harmony.

16. My children, no matter how long excreta sits in the sun, the stench will not go away unless it is exposed to the wind and open air. You may meditate for ages, but your *vasanas* won't be removed unless you live with your spiritual master. The master's grace is necessary. Only into the innocent mind will the master pour his or her grace.

17. To advance spiritually, it is necessary to have the attitude of total surrender to one's spiritual master. When a child is learning the alphabet, the teacher holds the child's finger and makes him or her trace letters in the sand. The teacher controls the movements of the child's finger. But if the child proudly thinks, "I know everything", and refuses to obey the teacher, how will he or she learn anything?

18.   My children, experiences are, indeed, the guru of each person. Sorrow is the teacher that brings us closer to God.

19.   We should have *bhaya bhakti* [reverential devotion] towards our spiritual master. At the same time, we should have a close relationship with the master and feel that he or she is our very own. The relationship should be like that of a mother and child. However much the mother spanks the child or pushes him or her away, the child continues to cling to her. Reverential devotion will help us to progress spiritually, but only through a close relationship with the master will there be any real benefit.

20.   My children, simply loving your spiritual master will not destroy your *vasanas*. You need devotion and faith based on the essential principles of spirituality. To develop this, dedication of body, mind and intellect is necessary. Complete faith and obedience to the master will be enough to eradicate the *vasanas*.

21.   Say that a seed has been sown in the shade of a tree. When it has begun to sprout, it should be transplanted; otherwise it won't grow properly. In the same way, the disciple should stay with the master for at least two or three years. After this, he or she should do spiritual practice in an isolated place. This is necessary for the disciple's spiritual progress.

22.   A real master will desire only the spiritual progress of the disciple. Tests and trials are given for the disciple's progress and to remove his or her weaknesses. The master may even blame the disciple for errors that he or she has not committed. Only those who steadily withstand such trials will progress.

23.   The real Guru can be known only through experience.

24.   An artificially incubated chicken cannot survive unless the ideal food and environment are provided. But a country-bred chicken can live on any food, under any circumstances. My children, spiritual

aspirants who live with a master are like country chickens. They will have the courage to overcome any situation. Nothing can enslave them. They will always carry with them the strength acquired from their close association with the master.

25.   A disciple may have a possessive attitude towards the master. This attitude cannot be easily destroyed. The disciple may desire the maximum amount of the master's love. When it seems as if they aren't getting this, some disciples may abuse and even leave the master. If a disciple wants the master's love, he or she must learn to serve selflessly.

26.   God's wrath can be appeased, but even God will not pardon the sin arising from contempt for the spiritual master.

27.   God and the spiritual teacher are within everyone. But in the beginning stages of spiritual practice, an external teacher is of utmost importance. After a certain point, however, this is no longer necessary.

From then on, the spiritual aspirant will be able to grasp the essential principles in everything, and thus move forward on his or her own. Until a child becomes aware of her goal, she studies her lessons out of fear of getting scolded by her parents and teachers. But once she becomes conscious of her goal, she studies of her own accord, foregoing sleep, movies and other things that she enjoys. The fear and reverence she has had until now towards her parents were not a weakness. My children, when the awareness of the goal dawns within you, the guru aspect will also awaken within you spontaneously.

28.   Even though a person may come in contact with a spiritual master, he will be accepted as a disciple only if he is fit to be a disciple. Without the master's grace, one cannot know the master. A person who is genuinely in search of Truth will be humble and possess a quality of simplicity. Only to such a soul will the master's grace flow. Those who are full of ego won't have any real access to the master.

29.   My children, you can say, "God and I are one and the same", but a disciple can never say, "My master and I are one." For the spiritual master is the one who awakens the divine 'I' within you. That unique greatness will always remain. The disciple should behave accordingly.

30.   Just as a hen protects her newly hatched chicks beneath her wing, the true master takes complete care of those who live according to his or her instructions. The master will point out even their silly mistakes and correct them then and there. The master won't allow even an iota of ego to develop in the disciple. In order to prune a person's pride, the master may at times act in an apparently cruel manner.

31.   When you see a blacksmith pounding a hot piece of iron against a hard rock with his hammer, you may think he is being cruel. The piece of iron may also feel that the blacksmith is the meanest brute in the world. But while dealing each blow, the blacksmith thinks only of the new form that is about

to emerge. My children, this is what a real spiritual teacher is like.

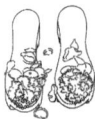

God

32. Many people ask, "Is there a God? If there is a God, where is He?" Ask those people, "Which originally came first, the hen or the egg?" or "Which came first, the coconut or the coconut tree?" Who can answer such questions? Beyond the coconut and the coconut tree, there is a living power that is the substratum of everything, a power beyond any possible description. That is God. My children, that primordial cause of everything is called God.

33. My children, to deny the existence of God is like using your tongue to say, "I have no tongue." Just as the tree is contained within a seed and butter within cream, God dwells in everything.

34. Even though the tree is latent in a seed, for the seed to be able to germinate it must have the humility to go down beneath the soil. There has to be an attitude of humbleness. And for an egg to hatch, it has to be incubated. A great deal of patience is neces-

sary. Butter can be separated from cream only when
the milk is set, made into curd, and then churned.
Even though God is all-pervading, strenuous effort
is necessary to realize him.

35.   Wherever there is ego and selfishness, God
cannot be seen. If, because of our sincere prayers,
God comes closer to us by one foot, he will move
away from us a thousand feet due to our selfishness.
You can jump into a well in no time, but it is difficult
to climb out of it. Similarly, God's grace, which is so
hard to obtain, can be lost in a moment.

36.   My children, even if one does penance during
many lifetimes, Self-realization is not possible without
innocent love and yearning for the Supreme Being.

37.   A woman is looked upon as a sister by her
brother, as a wife by her husband, and as a daughter
by her father. But no matter how anyone may see
her, she is just one person. Similarly, God is One. All

people look upon God in their own way, according to their attitudes.

38.   God can take any form. If you make a toy out of clay—for example an elephant or a horse—the clay will still always be clay. Different forms are latent in the clay. Similarly, any number of forms can be carved out of wood; but if you see the wood as wood, then wood is what it is. In the same way, God is all-pervading and has no attributes, but God reveals Him- or Herself to you according to your attitude.

39.   My children, just as water turns into ice and again melts back into water, God, by His will, can assume any form and then revert back to His pristine nature.

40.   Water flowing in different directions can be stored in a reservoir, if we build a dam. Electricity can be generated from the force of a waterfall produced in this way. Similarly, if the mind, now wandering among different sense objects, is trained to concentrate, the

vision of God can be attained through the power of that concentration.

41.   My children, once we take refuge in God, there is nothing to fear. God will look after everything. There is a children's game called tag. One child chases the others and tries to tag [touch] one of them. The others will run trying to evade the child's touch. If any of the children touch a designated 'safe' tree, they cannot be tagged. Likewise, if we hold onto God, no one can do anything to us.

42.   When a person looks at his father's portrait, he doesn't think about the artist or the paint; he is reminded of his father. In the same way, a devotee sees God, the Universal Father and Mother, in sacred images. Atheists may say it is the sculptor who is to be adored and not the image. But it is only because they do not have any concept of God and the principles behind the worship of icons that they say so, my children.

43.   There is no point in blaming God for the problems and unrighteousness in the world. God has shown us the right way and is not responsible for the miseries we create by not following that way. There is no point in finding fault with God. A mother will tell her child, "Do not touch fire or walk at the edge of a pond." If the child refuses to obey and burns a hand or falls into the pond, why blame the mother?

44.   Those who sit idly and say, "God will do everything", are sluggards. Our intelligence has been given to us by God so that we will use our power of discrimination in each action. If we simply say that God will look after everything, of what use is our intelligence?

45.   Some may argue, "If everything is God's will, isn't it also God who makes us commit mistakes?" It is meaningless to say this. The responsibility for any action that we do with a sense of ego rests on us ourselves, and not on God. If we really believe it is God who has made us commit a crime, we should also be

able to accept the sentence given to us by the judge as coming from God. Will we be able to do this?

46. My children, God-realization and Self-realization are the same. Expansiveness, perfect equanimity and the ability to love all—this is God-realization.

47. Even if we are loved by every being in the world, that love cannot give us an infinitesimal fraction of the bliss we experience from a momentary taste of God's love. So great is the bliss we get from God's love, my children, that no amount of love can be compared to it.

48. Just because you can't see God, can you say there is no God? There are many who have never seen their grandfather. Because of this, do they say that their father had no father?

49. As children, we ask countless questions. We learn so much from our mother and cooperate with her. As we grow a little older, we share our problems with our friends. As adults we confide in our husband

or wife. This is our *samskara* [inner disposition]. We should change this. We should be able to share our sorrows with something far vaster. We do have to share our sorrows with someone—we cannot progress without having a companion; but let that one companion and confidant be God.

50.   Today's friend may be tomorrow's foe. The only friend we can ever really trust and take refuge in is God.

51.   Does God gain anything by our believing in Him? Does the sun require the light of a candle? It is the believer who benefits from his or her faith. When we have faith and worship God in a temple and we witness the camphor being burned as an offering to God, it is we ourselves who experience concentration and peace.

52.   People of different religions follow different customs and have different places of worship, but God is one and the same. Even though milk is called "pal"

in Malayalam and "dhoodh" in Hindi, the substance and colour are exactly the same. The Christians worship Christ. Muslims call God Allah. The form of Krishna is not the same in Kerala as it is in northern India, where he is pictured wearing a turban, and so on. Each person understands and worships God according to his or her own culture and taste. The divine incarnations have portrayed the same God in different forms, according to the needs of the age and the different preferences of people.

53. In order to elevate yourself from identification with the body to the level of the glorious Self, you have to feel the same amount of desperation that a person who is trapped in a burning house, or someone who is drowning and cannot swim, feels to live. A seeker with that intensity won't have to wait long for the vision of God.

54. My children, having lost the key, we go to a blacksmith to get the lock opened. Similarly, to open

the lock of attraction and repulsion, we have to seek the key that lies in God's hands.

55.   God is the foundation of everything. Our faith in God will make love blossom within us. From this love, a sense of *dharma* will ensue, followed by a sense of justice. We will then experience peace. In our empathy we should be as eager to alleviate the suffering of others as we would be to apply a soothing salve to our own burned hand. This quality can be developed through real faith in God.

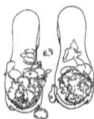

Mahatmas

Great Souls

56.   "The same Self that abides in all beings, abides in me as well. Nothing is different or separate from me. The suffering and hardships of others are my own." The person who realizes these truths through his or her own experience is a *jnani* [sage].

57.   The difference between a divine incarnation and a liberated individual soul can be compared to the difference between a singer who was born a musical prodigy and a person who has only recently learned how to sing. The former can master a song just by hearing it once, while for the latter it will take longer.

58.   Since everything is a part of God, everyone is a divine incarnation. However, those who do not know that they are a part of God and think, "I am

the body; this is *my* house and *my* property", are *jivas* [individual souls].

59.   The descent of God into a human form is called an *avatar* [divine incarnation]. The *avatar* has a sense of completeness which others do not have. Since the *avatar* is one with nature, his or her mind is not what we would normally call a mind. All minds are part of the Mind of the divine incarnation. The incarnation is the universal mind. He or she is beyond all pairs of opposites, such as purity and impurity, joy and sorrow.

60.   No limitations can bind a divine incarnation. An *avatar* of Brahman [the Absolute Being] is like an iceberg in the Ocean. The entirety of God's power cannot be contained in a human body that is five or six feet tall, but God can work at will through this small body. This is the unique quality of a divine incarnation.

61.   The divine incarnations are a great help in bringing people closer to God. It is for your sake only

that God assumes a form. An *avatar* is not the body, even though he or she may appear to be.

62. Wherever a *mahatma* goes, people gather around him or her. People are attracted to the *mahatma* like dust to a whirlwind. The *mahatma's* breath and even the breeze that touches his or her body benefits the world.

63. My children, Jesus was crucified and Krishna was killed by an arrow. These things happened only through their will. No one can approach a divine incarnation against his or her will. Krishna and Jesus could have burned those who opposed them to ashes, but they didn't. They incarnated in their bodies only to set an example for the world. They came to demonstrate the meaning of sacrifice.

64. A *sannyasi* [monk or nun] is one who has renounced everything. *Sannyasis* are those who endure and forgive the wrongdoings of others and lead them lovingly along the right path. They exem-

plify self-sacrifice. They are ever blissful and do not depend on external objects for their happiness. They revel in their own Self.

65.　A grown-up who walks beside a little child, holding his or her hand, will walk slowly taking small steps, lest the child should trip and fall. In the same way, to be able to uplift ordinary people, one first has to come down to their level. A seeker should never be a proud or pompous person, thinking, "I am a *sannyasi!*" He or she should set an example for the world.

66.　During His life, Sri Krishna played many roles—that of a cowherd boy, king, messenger, house-holder and charioteer. He never acted aloof, with the attitude, "I am the King!" Krishna taught how one should guide a person by being with that person according to his or her *samskara* [mental disposition]. Only such great souls can lead the world.

67.　There are some people who put on the ochre

robe and proudly declare, "I am a *sannyasi!*" They are like wild colocasia plants: the wild and cultivated varieties have a similar appearance, but the wild plant won't have any tubers when unearthed. Ochre is the colour of fire. Only those who have burnt their body-consciousness are fit to wear ochre.

Scriptures

68.   My children, the scriptures are the experiences of the *rishis* [Self-realized seers]. They cannot be grasped through the intellect. They can be realized only through experience.

69.   We need not learn all the scriptures; they are as vast as the ocean. We should pick up only the essential principles of the scriptures, like taking pearls from the sea. A person who is chewing a piece of sugarcane swallows only the juice and spits out the stalk.

70.   Only those who have done spiritual practice can grasp the subtle aspects of the scriptures.

71.   Scriptural studies alone will not lead to perfection. To cure a disease, reading the instructions on a medicine bottle is not enough. The medicine has to be ingested. Liberation cannot be attained by merely studying the scriptures. Practice is essential.

72.   It is better to both meditate and study the scriptures than to just mediate without the aid of any scriptural knowledge. If the mind of a person who has studied the scriptures gets agitated, he or she won't get depressed but will be able to regain inner strength by reflecting on the words of the scriptures. The words of the scriptures will help him or her to overcome weaknesses. Only those who combine spiritual practice with scriptural study can really serve the world selflessly.

73.   Studying the scriptures is necessary to a certain extent. A person who has studied agriculture can easily plant and cultivate a coconut tree. If there is any symptom of disease, he or she will be familiar with the appropriate remedies and know how to treat the tree.

74.   By merely drawing a picture of a coconut, we cannot quench our thirst. To get coconuts, we first have to plant and nurture the seedling of a coconut tree. In the same way, to experience all that is

described in the scriptures, we have to do spiritual practice.

75.   A person who spends his or her time merely learning the words of the scriptures, without doing any spiritual practice, is like a fool who tries to live in the blueprint of a house.

76.   If a traveller is familiar with the route he or she is travelling, the journey will be easy and he or she will quickly reach the destination. My children, the scriptures are the route maps that show us the path to our spiritual goal.

77.   A person who has chosen spiritual life shouldn't spend more than three hours a day studying the scriptures. The rest of the time should be spent repeating the mantra and meditating.

78.   Excessive indulgence in scriptural studies will prevent you from being able to meditate. The desire to teach people will always be present in your mind. You will think, "I am Brahman [the Supreme Being],

so why should I meditate?" Even if you try to sit for meditation, the mind will not allow it and will compel you to get up.

79. My children, what will you gain by spending your whole life studying the scriptures? To know what sugar tastes like, you don't have to eat a whole sack of it. A pinch will do.

80. The grain in the granary believes it is self-sufficient. It says, "Why should I bow down to the soil?" It does not realize that only if it comes out of the granary and germinates can it multiply and be of any use. If it remains in the granary, it will only become food for rats. People who study the scriptures without doing any spiritual practice are like the grain in the granary. Without having done any spiritual practice, how will they be able to use that knowledge properly? Such people are like parrots; they simply know how to repeat, "I am Brahman, I am Brahman."

Jnana, Bhakti and Karma Yoga

The Paths of Knowledge, Devotion and Action

81.   One person may like to eat raw jackfruit, someone else may like it boiled, while a third person prefers it fried. But though their tastes differ, the purpose of eating the fruit is to appease their hunger. In the same way, each person adopts a different path towards knowing God. My children, whatever path you choose to travel, the goal is the same: God-realization.

82.   Devotion without the proper understanding of the essentials of spirituality can only lead to attachment; it cannot grant you liberation. The jasmine creeper doesn't grow upwards; it branches out sideways by binding onto other trees.

83.   Knowledge without devotion is like eating stones.

84. To have true devotion rooted in the essentials of spirituality is to take refuge in the one God—who manifests as everything—with selfless love and without thinking that there are many separate Gods. Keeping the goal clearly in mind, we should move forward. If you want to go east, it is pointless to travel towards the west.

85. My children, the goal of life if Self-realization. Strive for that! Medicine should be applied to a wound only after it has been cleansed of all dirt. If the dirt remains, the wound won't heal and may get infected. In the same way, only after washing away the ego with the waters of devotion and love should supreme knowledge be imparted. Only then will you unfold spiritually.

86. If butter is melted, it won't go rancid. If it were to refuse to melt, saying proudly, "I am butter!" it would begin to stink in due course. My children, it is only through devotion that we can melt away the ego and other impurities.

87.   Some people ask why Mother places so much
importance on *bhakti yoga* [the path of devotion and
love]. My children, even Shankaracharya, who established the *Advaita* [non-dualistic] philosophy, eventually wrote the devotional piece, *Saundarya Lahari*.
Sage Vyasa, who composed the *Brahma Sutras*, was
content only after writing the *Srimad Bhagavatam*,
which glorifies Sri Krishna's life. Realizing that talking about *Advaita* and the philosophy of the *Brahma
Sutras* was of little use to ordinary people, Shankaracharya and Vyasa composed their devotional work.
One or two people out of a thousand may be able
to reach the goal through *jnana yoga* [the path of
knowledge and wisdom]. How could Amma discard
all the other seekers? For them, only *bhakti yoga* will
be beneficial.

88.   If we follow the path of devotion and love,
we can enjoy the fruit of bliss from the very beginning; whereas on other paths, the fruit is tasted only
towards the end. The path of devotion is like the
jackfruit tree, which bears fruit at its very base. With

other trees you may have to climb to the top to pluck the fruit.

89. Initially, we need to have *bhaya bhakti* [devotion with an element of awe and reverence] towards God. Later, that isn't necessary. When the state of supreme love has been reached, the element of awe and reverence disappears.

90. Everyone says that performing actions is enough. But to do actions in the right way, knowledge is necessary. Action without knowledge won't be right action.

91. Actions done with great attention will lead you to God. Be very attentive and alert, for only then can you gain concentration. Often, it is only after we have done something that we realize how we could have paid more attention. Having left the examination hall, the student thinks, "Oh, no! I should have answered in that way instead!" What is the use of dwelling on it afterwards?

92.   My children, every action should be done with great attention and alertness. Actions done without these qualities are useless. A spiritual aspirant can recall the details of tasks performed years ago because of the utmost attention with which those tasks were done. Even while engaged in seemingly trivial chores, we should do them with great attention.

93.   A needle may seem insignificant, but if you are using one you will be very careful; otherwise you won't be able to thread the needle. While sewing, if you are inattentive for even a moment, you could prick your finger. And you would never carelessly throw a needle on the ground, as it could pierce someone's foot, which would cause that person suffering. A spiritual aspirant should have that same attention while doing any work.

94.   We shouldn't talk while working. If we talk, we won't get any concentration; and working without concentration or attention is pointless. Whatever work we do, we shouldn't forget to repeat our mantra.

If the work is such that it isn't possible to repeat the mantra, then we should pray before beginning the work: "O God, it is through Your power that I am doing Your work. Give me the strength and capacity to do it well."

95.   Few are those who have the inner disposition inherited from former lives to be able to follow the path of *jnana* [supreme knowledge and wisdom]. However, those who have a true spiritual master can follow any path.

96.   First of all, external alertness and awareness is necessary. As long as you don't have this, it won't be possible for you to conquer your inner nature.

97.   A person who constantly thinks of God while doing any type of work is a real *karma yogi* and a true seeker. Such people see God in whatever work they do. Their minds are not on the work; their minds are resting in God.

Pranayama

Yogic Breathing Exercises

98.   *Pranayama* should be practiced with utmost care. While doing such exercises, the aspirant should sit with the spine erect. Ordinary diseases can be treated and cured, but not the disorders caused by the incorrect practice of *pranayama*.

99.   When *pranayama* is practiced, there will be some movement of the intestines in the lower abdominal area. Each *pranayama* exercise should be done for a specific amount of time. If these rules are violated, the digestive system will be irreparably damaged and food will pass through undigested. *Pranayama* should therefore be practiced only under the direct guidance of an adept, someone who knows exactly what needs to be done at each stage of one's spiritual progress, who can give the necessary instructions and also the appropriate herbal remedies if needed. It can be

dangerous to practice *pranayama* following only the guidance of books. No one should ever do this.

100. My children, the number of times *pranayama* should be performed is specified for each stage. If these specifications are not followed to the letter, the exercises can be dangerous. The effect will be like trying to stuff the contents of a ten-kilo sack into a five-kilo sack.

101. *Kumbhaka* is the stillness of breath that occurs when you get real concentration. You could say that breath is thought. Thus the rhythm of the breath will change according to the concentration of the mind.

102. Even without doing *pranayama*, *kumbhaka* can take place through devotion. It is enough to repeat the mantra continuously.

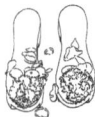

Meditation

103. Real education or knowledge is to make the mind concentrated.

104. You can meditate by fixing your attention on the heart centre or between the eyebrows. If you are unable to sit comfortably in one particular posture, you can meditate by fixing your attention on the heart. Meditation between the eyebrows is to be practiced only in the presence of a master, because while practicing this type of meditation your head may become hot and you may get a headache or feel dizzy. You could also experience insomnia. The master knows what is to be done if this should happen.

105. Meditation helps to free the mind from restlessness and tension. You don't have to believe in God in order to meditate. You can focus your mind on any part of the body or on any point. You can also

imagine that you are merging with infinity, just as a river merges into the ocean.

106. Happiness comes not from external objects but from the dissolution of mind. Through meditation, not only bliss, but also longevity, vitality, health, charm, strength and intelligence can be attained. But meditation should be practiced properly in solitude, with care and alertness.

107. It is possible to gain real concentration and mental purity by meditating on one of God's forms. Without our even being aware of it, the *sattvic* qualities of our Beloved Deity will develop within us. Even while sitting idle, do not let your mind wander. Wherever your gaze may fall, imagine you are seeing the form of your Beloved Deity there.

108. If you prefer to meditate on a flame, that is fine. Sit in a dark room and look for a long time at a burning candle or some other small flame. The flame should be steady. This flame can be meditated on by

visualizing it in your heart or between your eyebrows. After gazing at the flame for some time, you will see a light when you close your eyes. You can concentrate on that light as well. You can also meditate by imagining that your Beloved Deity is standing in the flame. But it is even better to visualize your Beloved Deity standing in a sacrificial fire, because then you can imagine that you are giving your ego, anger, jealousy—all your negative qualities—to your Beloved Deity to burn up in that sacrificial fire.

109. Don't stop your meditation just because the form isn't clear in your mind. You can visualize each part of your Beloved Deity within, going from head to toe. Give the Deity a ritual bath. Adorn the Deity with robes and ornaments. Feed Him or Her with your own hands. Through these visualizations, the form of your Beloved Deity won't fade from your mind.

110. My children, to compel the mind to meditate is like trying to submerge a piece of wood in water;

when you loosen your grip, the wood will immediately pop up. If it isn't possible for you to meditate, repeat your mantra. By chanting your mantra, you will help your mind become capable of meditating.

111. To begin with, meditation on a form is necessary. By meditating on a form, we fix our mind on the Beloved Deity. Regardless of how you meditate or what the object of your meditation may be, concentration is important. What is the use of sending a letter after affixing postal stamps, but without writing the proper address on it? This is what chanting a mantra or meditating without any concentration is like.

112. It is when we try to eliminate negative thoughts that they begin to cause trouble. When we previously indulged in such thoughts, we weren't bothered by them. It is when we adopt a different attitude that we become aware of our negativities. The negative thoughts were always there; we just didn't notice them. When those thoughts arise during meditation,

we should reason in this way: "Mind, what is the use of dwelling on those thoughts? Is it your goal to think about such things?" We should use our discrimination in that way. Total dispassion should be developed towards worldly thoughts and objects. Detachment should be cultivated and our love for God should grow.

113. My children, if you feel sleepy while meditating, take special care so that you don't become enslaved by the drowsiness. If you feel sleepy, get up and walk while chanting your mantra; then the *tamas* [lethargy] will go away. In the initial stages of meditation, all your *tamasic* qualities will surface. If you are vigilant, they will vanish in due course. When you feel sleepy, chant the mantra using a *mala* [rosary]. Holding the mala close to your chest, chant the mantra in an unhurried manner, with attention. When you meditate, don't lean against anything or move your legs.

114. No matter where you are, and whether you

are sitting or standing, your spine should always be straight. Don't meditate with your spine hunched. The mind is a thief, always waiting for the opportunity to steal you away. If you lean on anything, you may fall asleep without being aware of it.

115. A minimum of three years is required to get the form of your meditation properly fixed within. Initially, by looking at a picture of your Beloved Deity, you should strive to attain concentration. After spending ten minutes looking at the form of your meditation, you can meditate for ten minutes with your eyes closed. If you continue practicing in this way, in due course the form will become clear.

116. If the form fades from your mind during meditation, try to visualize it again. You can also imagine coiling and uncoiling the rope of *japa* around your Beloved Deity, from head to foot and foot to head. This will help you to fix your mind on the form.

117. Talking right after meditation is like spending

all one's hard-earned money on peanuts. The power acquired through meditation will be completely wasted.

118. At night the atmosphere is calm, for at that time the birds, animals and worldly people are all subdued by sleep. There are, therefore, fewer worldly thought waves in the atmosphere at night. Flowers bloom in those late hours. At that time the atmosphere has a unique, energizing effect. If you meditate then, your mind will easily become one-pointed and be absorbed in meditation for a long time. Night is the time when the yogis remain awake.

119. When we meditate on a form, we are actually meditating on our own true Self. At midday, when the sun is directly overhead, there is no shadow. Meditation on a form is like this: when we reach a certain stage the form of our meditation will drop off and we will merge with That. Having reached the stage of perfection, there is no shadow, no duality, no illusion.

The Mantra

120. If mantras had no power, then words wouldn't have any power either. If a person is angrily told, "Get out!" the effect will be entirely different from what it would be if he is politely asked, "Please leave." Don't those words create different reactions in a listener?

121. We chant a mantra to make our minds pure, not to satisfy God. Of what benefit is a mantra to God?

122. Don't trouble the intellect by pondering the meaning of your mantra; it is enough just to chant it. You may have come to the ashram by bus, car, boat or train, but once you have arrived, do you waste your time thinking about the vehicle? Being aware of the goal is all that is needed.

123. There are different types of *diksha* [initiation]: *diksha* through a *mahatma's* glance, touch or thought, or with a mantra. Mantra initiation should be received from a *satguru* [realized master]. If the

teacher is a fake, the result will be like using a dirty filter to purify water; the water will become even more impure.

124. My children, even after you have boarded the bus and bought the ticket, you shouldn't be careless. The ticket should be kept safely. If you can't show your ticket when the ticket inspector comes, he will throw you off the bus. Similarly, just because you have been given a mantra, don't think your work ends there. Only if a mantra is used properly will it take you to the goal.

125. My children, it is difficult to row a boat through water covered with lily pads. The boat will move with greater ease if the lily pads are removed. In the same way, it will be easier for you to meditate if, by chanting the mantra, you remove the impurities of the mind.

126. It is important to chant the mantra with awareness. As you repeat your mantra, try to avoid all other

thoughts. Care should be taken to fix the mind either on the form of your meditation or on the letters of the mantra.

127. My children, always chant your mantra. The mind should be trained to repeat the mantra incessantly, so that no matter what you are doing, the mantra is being chanted. A spider spins its web wherever it goes. In the same way, while doing each action, we should mentally continue doing *japa*.

128. However much we feed and stroke a cat, the moment we divert our attention it will steal food. This is what the mind is like. Try to tame and concentrate the mind by always repeating your mantra. While walking, sitting or working, the mantra should continue to flow, like oil being poured from one vessel to another.

129. In the initial stages of your spiritual practice, in addition to contemplating a form, repeating a mantra is also necessary. Don't worry if the form isn't clear

in your mind; it is enough if you continue chanting the mantra at that time. As progress is made, the mind will eventually get fixed on the form and the repetition of the mantra will naturally slow down.

130. My children, it is not necessary to chant all of the different *Sahasranamas* [A *Sahasranama* is a collection of names that describe different aspects of a deity]. Any one of them is enough. Everything is contained in each *Sahasranama*.

131. My children, whenever your mind is restless, repeat your mantra. Otherwise your restlessness will only increase. When the mind isn't calm it resorts to external objects, and when that isn't fruitful, the mind will turn to something else. External objects cannot give you peace. Only by focusing on God and chanting your mantra will your peace of mind be restored. Reading spiritual books is also beneficial.

132. Children learn to count by using an abacus. With this method they are able to learn quickly. In

the same way, when beginning to learn to control the mind, it is good to use a *mala* when you repeat your mantra. Later you will no longer need a *mala*. If you repeat the mantra regularly, the mantra will become a part of you. Even while sleeping you will continue to repeat the mantra without being aware of it.

133. However much we meditate and repeat the mantra, if we do not love God, our spiritual practice will be fruitless. No matter how hard we row a boat against the current, it will only inch its way forward; but if we put up a sail, the boat will pick up speed. Love for God is like a sail that helps us to move rapidly towards the goal. This will help us to reach the goal very easily.

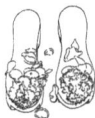

Devotional Singing

134. In this *kali yuga* [dark age] it is very effective to repeat a mantra and to sing devotional songs. The same money that was gained by selling 1,000 acres in the olden days, can be gained today by selling just one acre. This is a sign of the *kali yuga*. If even as little as five minutes of concentration can be attained, my children, that is certainly a great asset.

135. At dusk, when day and night meet, the atmosphere is full of impure vibrations. For a seeker this is the best time to meditate. Good concentration can be attained at this time. If you are not doing spiritual practice during sundown, many worldly thoughts will appear. This is why it is said that devotional songs should be sung loudly at dusk. The singing will purify both the singer and the atmosphere.

136. Because the atmosphere in the *kali yuga* is full of sounds, devotional singing is more effective than meditation for gaining concentration. Quiet

surroundings are necessary for meditation. It is for this reason that bhajan singing is more effective. By singing loudly, we overcome other distracting sounds and achieve concentration. Meditation is something that is beyond concentration. This is the progression: bhajan singing, concentration and then meditation. My children, to meditate is to constantly remember God.

137. To sing devotional songs without concentration is a waste of energy. But if they are sung with one-pointedness of mind, it will benefit the singer, the listeners and nature as well. In due course, such songs will help awaken the listener's mind.

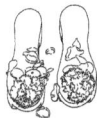

Vows and Other Spiritual Observances

138. My children, just as the shore stops the waves of the sea, observing vows on the spiritual path controls the waves of the mind.

139. On certain days [e.g. *ekadasi* and full moon days], there are more negative vibrations in the atmosphere. During such times, it is good to observe a vow of silence and to eat only fruits. Fruits that are covered with peel are hardly affected by atmospheric impurities. On those days especially it is important to do spiritual practice. We should then try to attain more concentration, whether our thoughts are spiritual or worldly.

140. It is good for a seeker to purge the stomach at least twice a month. The accumulated faeces in the intestines create agitation and negativity in the mind. By purging, we clear not only the body but the mind as well.

141. Once a week, take a vow of silence and eat only fruit. Devote that day to meditation and to chanting your mantra. This will benefit your body, your mind, and your spiritual practice.

142. It is helpful for a seeker who does regular spiritual practice to fast occasionally. This will make the mind and body fit for meditation. However, those who do strenuous work as well as meditation should not fast completely. They should eat as much as they require. Fruits are very good.

143. Seekers should carefully choose every word they utter. They should speak in a subdued tone so that their listeners will be able to hear only if they keep their minds and senses very attentive.

144. My children, a person who is sick has to observe certain restrictions in order to get well. A seeker also has to follow certain restrictions until he or she reaches the goal; for example, talking as little as

possible, taking vows of silence, and controlling the diet.

145. The observance of vows is not a sign of weakness. Only wooden planks that are bent are useful for building a boat, and they have to be heated in order to bend. Similarly, by observing spiritual disciplines, we bring the mind under control. And without taming the mind, we cannot control the body.

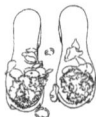

Patience and Self-Discipline

146. My children, spiritual life is possible only for a person who has patience.

147. Spiritual progress can't be measured by simply observing someone's external actions. A person's spiritual advancement can be known to a certain extent by his or her reactions to adverse situations.

148. How can a person who gets angry about petty things lead the world? Only someone who has patience can guide others. The ego should be completely annihilated. No matter how many people sit in a chair, it doesn't complain. In the same way, regardless of how many people get angry with us, we should develop the strength to endure and forgive. Otherwise there is no point in doing spiritual practice.

149. If you get angry, much of the power you have gained through your spiritual practice will be lost.

While a vehicle is running smoothly, not much energy is dissipated; but if we keep stopping and starting, more fuel will be spent. In the same way, anger drains your power through every pore of your body.

150. Though we can't see that the fuel is decreasing, when a cigarette lighter has been used a certain amount of times, its fuel will be spent. This can be known but cannot be seen clearly. Similarly, the energy we have acquired through good thoughts can be lost in many ways. For instance, when we get angry, whatever we have gained through our spiritual practice will be lost. When we talk, our energy is spent through the mouth; but anger also dissipates energy through the eyes and ears and through every pore of the body.

151. It is essential for a spiritual aspirant to keep a strict timetable. Have a routine of chanting the mantra and meditating at the same time and for a set duration every day. Develop the habit of doing

spiritual practice at a fixed time. This habit will lead you forward.

152. Those who have grown accustomed to drinking tea at a particular time every day have to drink tea at that time, otherwise they will feel restless and run to get their tea. Those who have a regular timetable for spiritual discipline will automatically follow it at the fixed times.

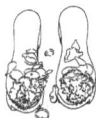

Humility

153. In a cyclone, large trees are uprooted and buildings collapse. But no matter how strong the cyclone is, it cannot damage a lowly blade of grass. This is the greatness of humility, my children.

154. Humbleness is not a sign of weakness. We should have the greatness to bow down even to the grass. If you come to a river and are unwilling to bow down to the water (i.e. go beneath the surface of the water) and wash yourself, your body will remain dirty. By refusing to be humble towards others, the spiritual aspirant prevents his or her ignorance from being destroyed.

155. Human beings have the arrogance to claim that by simply pressing a button, they could burn the world to ashes. But to press that button, one's hand has to move. We don't think about the Power behind that movement.

156. Humanity claims to have conquered the world. We don't even have the capacity to count the grains of sand beneath our feet; yet such small fry claim to have conquered the world!

157. Suppose someone gets angry with you for no reason. As a spiritual aspirant, you should respond with an attitude of humility towards that person, realizing that what is happening is a play of God, enacted in order to test you. Only if you succeed in doing this can it be said that you have gained the benefit of your meditation.

158. Even while someone is cutting down a tree, the tree provides that person with shade. This is what a spiritual person should be like. Only someone who prays for the welfare of others, even for those who make him or her suffer, can truly be called a spiritual person.

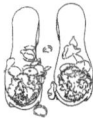

Selfishness and Desire

159. The ego arises out of desire and selfishness. It does not appear naturally, but is created.

160. Suppose you go to collect the money that someone owes you. You expect to get two hundred rupees, but you are given only fifty. This makes you so angry that you pounce on the other person and beat him or her up. Afterwards you are taken to court. Wasn't your anger the result of being denied the expected amount? When you receive your punishment, what is the use of blaming God? Because of our expectations we get angry, and because of desires we suffer. This is the result of running after desires.

161. The wind of God's grace cannot lift us up as long as we are carrying the load of our ego and desires. The load should be reduced.

162. Many flowers grow on a tree that has shed all of its leaves; on other trees there are flowers only here

and there. My children, when we are totally free from
negative tendencies, such as selfishness, egoism and
jealousy, we will attain the vision of God.

163. A spiritual aspirant shouldn't have the slightest
trace of selfishness. Selfishness is like a worm sucking
the nectar out of flowers. If the worm is allowed to
remain, it will infest the fruits of the tree, and then
the fruits will be useless. In the same way, if your
selfishness is allowed to grow, it will gnaw away all
your good qualities.

164. There is a great difference between the desires
of a spiritual aspirant and the desires of a worldly
person. The desires of worldly people will wash over
them like waves, one after the other, and trouble
them. There is no end to their desires. But for a
spiritual seeker there is only one desire, and once
that desire is fulfilled, there are no more desires.

165. Even the "selfishness" of a spiritual person
benefits the world. There were two children living

in a village. Both of them were given some seeds by a visiting *sannyasi*. The first child roasted his seeds and ate them, thus appeasing his hunger. He was a worldly person. The second child sowed his seeds in the ground and thereby produced a lot of grain, which he gave to people who were hungry. Even though both children had the initial selfishness to accept what was given to them, the second one's attitude benefited many people.

166. There is only one Self. It is all-pervasive. When our minds expand, we can merge with That. Then our selfishness and ego will be gone forever. To those established in that state of supreme consciousness, everything is equal.

My children, without wasting a single moment, serve others and help the poor. Serve the world selflessly, without expecting anything in return.

167. A small selfishness can get rid of a big selfishness. A small poster saying "Stick no bills" will keep

the rest of the wall clean. This is what being selfish for God is like.

Diet

168. Without forsaking the taste of the tongue, the taste of the heart cannot be enjoyed.

169. You cannot say, "This food should be eaten, and that should not be eaten." The effect of a diet will vary according to the climatic conditions. The type of food that is avoided here [in south India] may be good for you in the Himalayas.

170. When you sit down for a meal, you should pray to God before you begin to eat. This is why a mantra is chanted before eating. The proper time to test our patience is when we have food before us.

171. An ascetic need not wander in search of food. The spider weaves its web and then stays there. It doesn't go anywhere to hunt for food, because its prey will get entangled in the web. In the same way, food will come to the ascetic. But for this to really happen, he or she has to have totally surrendered to God.

172. Diet has a great deal of influence on our character. Stale foods, for example, will increase our *tamas* [lethargy].

173. In the initial stages of an aspirant's spiritual practice, he or she should exercise control with respect to food. An uncontrolled diet will produce bad tendencies. When seeds are first sown, care should be taken not to let the crows peck at them. Later, when the seed has grown into a tree, any bird can come sit in the tree or build a nest in it. From now on, your diet should be strictly controlled and you should do your spiritual practice regularly. At a later stage, hot, sour and non-vegetarian food can be eaten, and they won't affect you. But even though Amma has told you that at a later stage any food can be eaten, don't consume such foods even then. You should live as an example for the world, so that others can learn by observing you. Even if we ourselves are not sick, we should refrain from eating hot or sour foods in front of a person who has jaundice. We

should exercise self-control in order to help others to become good.

174. People say that to stop drinking tea or to quit smoking is easy, yet many people are unable to stop. How is it possible for people to control the mind if they can't even control such silly things? Those trivial obstacles first have be overcome. If you can't ford a small river, how will you ever cross the ocean?

175. In the beginning, a spiritual aspirant shouldn't eat anything from shops [restaurants]. While adding each ingredient, the shopkeeper's only thought will be how to make more profit. While making tea, shopkeepers think, "Is this much milk really needed? Perhaps the sugar can be reduced." They will always be thinking of ways to reduce the quantity in order to boost their profit. The vibration of those thoughts will affect the seeker.

There was a *sannyasi* who was not in the habit of reading newspapers. Yet one day after eating in someone's home, an intense desire to read the newspaper sprang up in him. From that day on, he started dreaming about newspapers and the news. Upon inquiring, he discovered that the cook in the house he had visited had been reading the newspaper while preparing the food. The cook's attention had not been on the cooking but on the newspaper, and those thought waves had affected the *sannyasi*.

176. Never overeat. Half the stomach should be for food, a quarter for water, and the remaining portion for the movement of air. The less food you eat, the more mental control you will have. Do not sleep or meditate immediately after eating; if you do, you won't be able to digest the food properly.

177. Once love for God develops, you are like a person suffering from a fever. If you have a high fever, you won't find food tasty. Even sweet food will have a bitter taste. The same thing happens when you love God; your appetite spontaneously decreases.

Brahmacharya

Living as a celibate

178. Hot and sour food is harmful for *brahmacharya*. Too much salt shouldn't be used either. A limited amount of sugar is harmless. It isn't good to consume yoghurt at night, and milk should be used only in moderation. Milk for drinking should be mixed with an equal amount of water and then boiled. Also, too much oil should be avoided or else the body's fat content will increase, which will create an increase in semen.

179. Too much tasty food should not be eaten. If the desire for tasty food increases, temptations of the body will also increase. It is better not to eat in the morning, and only a small quantity should be eaten at night.

180. There is no need to be afraid of the emission of semen during sleep. Haven't you seen cow dung

being burnt and mixed with water to make sacred ash? A cloth wick is placed in the vessel with one end hanging outside the rim. The excess water then runs out through the wick, but the essence isn't lost. Only after the water has been expelled will sacred ash be produced.

However, special care should be taken so that emission doesn't occur while dreaming.

181. My children, whenever it is felt that emission will take place, you should immediately get up and meditate or repeat your mantra. Whether it happens or not, the next day you should do spiritual practice and fast the whole day. Bathing in a river or in the sea is good for *brahmacharya*.

182. During certain months and on certain days, the atmosphere will be very impure. At such times, however much care is taken, emission may occur. Mid-July to mid-August is such a period.

183. Due to the heat generated by the concentration

of the mind, the power of *brahmacharya* is transformed into *ojas* [subtle vital energy]. If a worldly person observes celibacy, he or she should perform spiritual practice as well, or the power of *brahmacharya* will not be converted into *ojas*.

The Seeker and Spiritual Practice

184. My children, our attitude towards everything in Creation should be free from expectation. This is the purpose of spiritual practice.

185. There is no shortcut to attaining the vision of God. Though sugar candy is sweet, no one swallows it whole; if one did, it would cut one's throat. It should be slowly dissolved and then swallowed. Similarly, spiritual practice should be performed regularly and with patience.

186. There is not much use in meditating or chanting a mantra without feeling any love for God. On the other hand, those who think they will start doing spiritual practice as soon as they develop love for God are idlers. They are like a person who is waiting for the waves of the ocean to subside before getting into the water.

187. Through spiritual practice, we get *shakti* [energy] and the body is freed from disease. It will also be possible to perform action on any occasion without getting easily exhausted.

188. Your Beloved Deity will take you to the threshold of realization. When you come to the ashram, if you travel by bus to Vallickavu junction, you can then walk the remaining distance to the jetty, can't you? Similarly, the Deity will bring you to the gate of *akhanda satchidananda* [undivided Existence-Awareness-Bliss].

189. My children, before we can set out to teach the world, we have to gain the strength to do so. Those who go to the Himalayas will bring woollen clothing to protect them from the cold. In the same way, before entering the world, the mind should be made strong so that it won't be disturbed by any adversities. This is possible only through spiritual practice.

190. Real *satsang*[1] is the union of the individual soul with the supreme Self.

191. A person who has a craving for dates will risk climbing up a wasp-infested tree to obtain the fruit. Similarly, a person who has *lakshya bodha* [a strong commitment to achieve the spiritual goal] will overcome any adverse circumstances.

192. In the beginning it is beneficial for a spiritual aspirant to go on a pilgrimage. A journey with some hardships will help him or her understand the nature of the world. But those who haven't yet gained enough strength through their spiritual practice will break down before the trials and tribulations of the world. So what is required is continuous spiritual practice while staying in one place, without wasting any time.

193. The perfection of the *asana* [sitting posture] is the first thing a spiritual aspirant needs to develop.

---

[1] See glossary

This is not always easy to achieve. Each day, sit for five minutes longer than you did the day before. In this way, it will gradually become possible for you to sit for two or three hours at a stretch. If you acquire this sort of patience, then everything will come easily.

While we walk, sit or bathe, we should always imagine that our Beloved Deity is walking with us and is smiling at us. We should imagine that the form of our Beloved Deity is standing in the sky, and we should pray to him or her.

194. My children, if you cry for God for five minutes, it is equal to one hour of meditation. When you cry, the mind easily becomes absorbed in the remembrance of God. If it isn't possible for you to cry, pray in this way: "Oh, God, why am I unable to cry for You?"

195. A spiritual aspirant shouldn't cry for fleeting things, but only for Truth. Our tears should be shed for God alone. A spiritual aspirant should never be

weak. He or she has to shoulder the burden of the whole world.

196. Our feelings can be expressed in three ways: through words, through tears and through laughter. My children, only when your mental impurities are washed away by torrential tears of yearning for the Divine will you be able to really smile with an open heart. Only then will true happiness be experienced.

197. Spiritual practice is essential. Even though the plant is contained within the seed, only when the seed is cultivated, fertilized and properly cared for will it sprout and bring forth flowers and seeds. In the same way, even through the Supreme Truth resides in all beings, it will shine forth only through spiritual practice.

198. If a seedling is planted but not properly cared for, it will wither. It should be tended regularly. After it has grown into a healthy plant, even if its top is cut off, it will still continue to grow with many new

shoots. However difficult the rules may be, in the beginning stages a spiritual aspirant should adhere to them. Only then will he or she progress.

199. It is good for a spiritual aspirant to visit slums, hospitals, etc., at least once a month. For this will help him or her understand the nature of life's miseries and will make the mind compassionate.

200. When milk is set to become curd, it shouldn't be disturbed. Only then can we make butter out of it. In the beginning stages of spiritual practice, solitude is necessary.

201. When seeds are sown, care should be taken so that the hens do not eat them. Later when the seeds have sprouted, they will be safe. In the beginning stages of spiritual practice, a spiritual aspirant shouldn't mix much with anyone. Devotees who are householders should be especially careful about this. Don't waste time chatting with your neighbours.

Whenever you have time, sit by yourself and repeat your mantra, meditate or sing devotional songs.

202. In the depths of the ocean there are no waves; the waves appear only on the surface. At the bottom of the ocean everything is calm. Those who have attained perfection are peaceful. It is the ones who have some superficial knowledge, who have read just two or three spiritual books, who make a hue and cry.

203. The waves of the sea cannot be destroyed. Likewise, the thoughts of the mind cannot be eliminated. Once the mind becomes deep and expansive, the thought waves naturally subside.

204. My children, both the real and the unreal are contained within the seed. When a seed is sown, the husk will crack and dissolve into the soil. It is the essence of the seed that sprouts and grows. Similarly, both the real and the unreal are within us. If we live adhering to what is real, nothing will bother us—we

will become expansive. If we cling to the unreal, we won't be able to grow.

205. When you know the Truth, the whole world is your wealth. You do not see anything as separate from your own Self.

206. It is through your deeds that your worth can be determined. You may be educated and have a good job, but if you steal, no one will respect you. Your progress as a spiritual aspirant can be judged by your deeds.

207. Haven't you seen soldiers and policemen standing like statues even in the pouring rain and the hot sun? Similarly, whether a spiritual aspirant is standing, sitting or lying down, he or she should be perfectly still. There shouldn't be any unnecessary movements of the hands, legs or body. To manage this, it is helpful to imagine that the body is dead. Eventually, through practice, stillness will become a habit.

208. A man who is rowing a boat out to sea will row hard, completely focused on what he is doing. The people standing on the shore watching will encourage him by waving their arms and shouting. But the rower won't pay any attention to them. His only thought is to get the boat to the point where it will be beyond the grasp of the waves. Once the waves have been traversed, there is nothing to fear. Then, if necessary, he can even rest on the oars for a while.

Similarly, you are now out among the waves. Without allowing yourself to be distracted by anything, proceed with great alertness, keeping the goal before you. Only then will you reach your destination.

209. A spiritual aspirant should be very careful regarding the opposite sex. Like a whirlwind, only after it has swept you away and flung you down do you realize the danger.

210. My children, water has no colour. A lake or a pond has the colour that is reflected onto it by the sky. Similarly, it is due to a person's own nega-

tive character that he or she sees the bad in others. Always try to see the good side in everyone.

211. A spiritual aspirant shouldn't go to weddings or funerals. At a wedding, everyone, young and old alike, will be thinking of marriage. And at a funeral everyone is grieving over the loss of a mortal being. The thought waves that are present on both occasions are harmful to a spiritual aspirant. The vibrations will enter the subconscious mind and will make the seeker restless for things that are unreal.

212. A spiritual person should be like the wind. Without any bias, the wind blows over fragrant flowers as well as over foul-smelling excreta. In the same way, a spiritual aspirant shouldn't be attached to those who show him or her affection, or feel any malice towards those who abuse him or her. To a spiritual aspirant, everyone is equal. He or she sees God in everything.

213. It isn't good to sleep during the day because

when you wake up you will feel exhausted. This is because during the day the atmosphere is full of impure thought waves, whereas at night it is far less polluted. In the mornings when we get up after a night's sleep, we feel energetic. For this reason, a spiritual aspirant should meditate more at night. It is enough to meditate for five hours at night instead of ten during the day.

214. My children, whatever sorrows you have, look at nature and imagine your Beloved Deity's form in the trees, the mountains and other objects, and share your feelings with those parts of nature. Or you can imagine that your Beloved Deity is standing in the sky, and talk to Him or Her. Why would you want to share your sorrows with anyone else?

215. If we are standing close to someone who is talking, what that person says will create a certain aura around us. Through bad company, a negative aura will be formed, causing an increase of impure

thoughts. This is why it is said that *satsang* [holy company and spiritual discourses] is necessary.

216. When a sculptor looks at a piece of wood or stone, he or she sees only the image that can be carved out of it; whereas everyone else will see only wood or stone. Similarly, a seeker should be able to discern the eternal in everything. We should understand what is eternal and what is fleeting, and live with caution. We should cling to that which is eternal alone. My children, only God is eternal Truth. Everything else is false and non-existent. Worldly matters do not last. That which is eternal is God.

217. My children, one isn't tempted by the nudity of a child. It should be possible to look at everyone in that same spirit. Everything depends on the mind.

218. A spiritual aspirant should be very careful in the beginning. The most favourable times for meditation are in the morning until 11 A.M. and after 5:00 P.M. Immediately after your meditation, you should lie

down in *savasana* [the corpse pose] for at least ten minutes before getting up. Even if you meditate for only one hour, you should be silent for at least half an hour afterwards. Only those who do this will get the full benefit of their meditation.

219. When medicine has been injected, it will take some time before it spreads throughout the body. In the same way, after doing spiritual practice, some time should be spent in silence. If, after two hours of meditation, you immediately start talking about worldly things or make any loud sounds, you will not have gained anything by your meditation, even if you have spent years meditating.

220. If someone is wasting your time talking about unnecessary things, you should either repeat your mantra and contemplate your Beloved Deity, or think of the person who is talking to you as your Beloved Deity. You can also draw a triangle on the ground and imagine your Deity standing there. Then take some small stones and, imagining that they are flowers,

offer them at the feet of your Deity. We should talk to others only about spiritual matters. Those who feel drawn to spirituality will listen; the rest will soon leave us. In this way we don't have to waste our time.

221. My children, even the breath of a spiritual aspirant is enough to purify the atmosphere—such is its power. It may take some time, but this fact will definitely be discovered by science. Only then will people really believe it.

222. Human beings are not the only ones with the capacity of speech. Animals, birds and plants also have this power. We just don't have the ability to understand them. Those who have experienced a vision of the Self know all these things.

223. Water stagnates in ditches and ponds. Germs and insects like to breed there, causing many people to become afflicted with disease. The remedy for this is to make the water flow, by connecting it to a river. Similarly, nowadays people live with the ego

of 'I' and 'mine.' Their impure thoughts cause suffering to many people. It is our goal to broaden their narrow minds and to guide them to the Supreme Being. Towards this end, each one of us should be prepared to endure some sacrifice. But only with the power acquired through spiritual practice can we lead people.

224. Equanimity is *yoga* [union with God]. Once equanimity is attained, a continuous flow of grace will be experienced. Then, spiritual practice is no longer needed.

The Spiritual Aspirant and His or Her Family

225. My children, it is our duty to look after our parents if there is no one else to look after them. This is our duty even if we have chosen to follow the spiritual path. We should look upon our parents as our own Self and serve them as such.

226. If your parents are a hindrance to your spiritual life, it is not necessary to obey them.

227. Is it right to take to spiritual life even if it means disobeying your parents? Suppose you have to go to a far place to study medicine, but your parents do not approve. If you disobey your parents and go away to study and become a doctor, you will be able to save the lives of thousands of people, including your parents. Your one selfishness would turn out to benefit the world. There is no harm in this. Had you obeyed your parents and not studied, you could have looked

after them, but you wouldn't have been able to save their lives.

Only a spiritual seeker can selflessly love and serve the world and truly save others. Didn't Shankaracharya and Ramana Maharshi each also come to his mother's rescue?[2]

228. Once we have chosen to lead a spiritual life, we should give up our attachment to our family. Otherwise it won't be possible for us to progress. No matter how hard you row a boat, if the boat is anchored it won't move forward. Having dedicated our lives to

---

[2] Both of these great saints left home at an early age, but eventually went back to their parents. After a separation of many years, Shankaracharya went to his mother as she lay on her deathbed and blessed her with a vision of God. And when Ramana Maharshi had completed his spiritual practices and had a proper place to stay, he invited his mother to come and stay with him. She lived with her son in Thiruvannamalai until she died, and with his grace she merged with God at the time of her death.

God, we should have strong faith that God will look after our families.

229. My children, who is our true mother and who is our true father? Are they the ones who gave birth to our bodies? Never. They are only our foster parents. A real mother or father is one who can give life to a dying child, and only God can do this. We should always remember this.

230. A small plant that grows in the shade of a big tree will grow comfortably for some time. But when the tree sheds its leaves, everything changes for the little plant, and it soon withers away in the hot sun. The situation of those who live in the 'shade' of their family can be compared to this.

For Householders

231. Nowadays the love and devotion we have for God are like the love we have for our neighbours. When the neighbours don't live according to our wants, we fight with them. We have the same attitude towards God. If God doesn't fulfil all our petty requests, we stop praying and repeating our mantra.

232. Think of how much we are prepared to toil to win a court case! And we will stand in a long queue to get into a cinema. Our desire to see the movie is so intense that we don't even mind if people shove and push. We willingly endure all these hardships for the sake of some external happiness. If such sacrifices were made for spiritual life, that would be enough for us to reach eternal bliss.

233. Suppose a small child cuts her hand. If we try to comfort her by saying, "You are not the body, mind or intellect", she won't understand anything and will only cry. Likewise, it is no use telling a worldly per-

son, "You are not the body—you are Brahman. The world is unreal." Perhaps some small change can be brought about by this attitude, but he or she should really be given practical advice that can be applied to daily life.

234. My children, many of those who take sudden delight in spirituality after hearing a spiritual discourse will not actually be able to lead a stable spiritual life. However long one may press a spring together, as soon as the pressure is released, it will resume its original shape.

235. Nowadays it seems that no one has time to go to temples or ashrams or to do any spiritual practice. But if our own child is sick, we are prepared to wait for any length of time in the waiting area of a hospital, without getting any sleep. To gain just one foot of land, we will wait outside the courthouse for any number of days in the rain or sun, without even thinking of our husband, wife or children. We can spend hours waiting in a crowded shop to buy a

needle for a few paise, but we have no time to pray to God. My children, for those who love God, time for spiritual practice will automatically be available.

236. Who says there is no time to repeat the mantra? You can chant your mantra while walking, repeating the mantra once for every step or so that you take. You can also do your spiritual practice while travelling in a bus, imagining the Beloved Deity's form in the sky. Or else, repeat your mantra in the bus, with your eyes closed. If the mantra is chanted in this way, no time will be wasted, for the mind will not get entangled in roadside attractions. It should also be possible for you to repeat your mantra while doing any household chores. Those who are interested will always make time for spiritual practices.

237. If a person cannot sleep, there are sleeping pills. For forgetting sorrow, intoxicants like liquor and marijuana are readily available. There are also cinemas. Because of these things, hardly anyone is searching for God nowadays. But people aren't

aware that those intoxicants are destroying them. When such intoxicants are consumed, the water content of the brain is reduced. It is then that one feels intoxicated. Through continuous use of such substances, the nerves in the body start to contract due to dehydration. After some time, one will be affected by shaking and tiredness, and not even be able to walk. Losing his or her vitality and brilliance, the person will gradually degenerate. Children born to such parents will have the same illness as their parents.

238. My children, it is the mind that needs to be air-conditioned, not the room. Having air-conditioned their rooms, people even commit suicide in them. Would they do this if luxury items gave them any real happiness? True happiness is not to be found on the outside—only within.

239. When a dog gets a bone, he chews it. When blood oozes, the dog thinks it is coming from the bone. It doesn't know it is licking its own blood

coming from its own injured gums. This is what the experience of seeking happiness from external things is like.

240. We wouldn't make a fence by chopping branches from a high-yielding fruit tree. Only less useful trees are used for that purpose. If the value of life were understood, it wouldn't be wasted on sensual pleasures.

241. There is no particular time when a householder should begin spiritual life. We should start when we feel the renunciation to do so. We don't have to force this urge upon ourselves; it will come of its own accord. An egg that is being incubated shouldn't be pecked open; it should be allowed to open by itself. If, for example, your spouse and children can live comfortably without you and you have the spirit of renunciation, then you can give up everything and embark on a life of renunciation. But afterwards you shouldn't entertain any thoughts about your home.

242. In the olden days, people taught their children the truth of what is permanent and what is fleeting. They taught them that the aim of life is God-realization. The children were given an education that enabled them to understand who they were. Nowadays parents encourage their children only to earn money. What is the result? The child doesn't know the parent and the parent doesn't know the child. There is enmity and fighting between them. They may even kill each other for selfish reasons.

243. My children, God-realization is not possible without doing spiritual practice; but hardly anyone is ready to strive. In factories, nightshift workers work all night without getting any sleep. They do not grow careless saying that they feel sleepy. If they are not careful, they could lose a hand or a leg, and then they will also lose their job. This sort of alertness and dispassion is also necessary in spiritual matters.

244. At dusk, a small child may worry, thinking, "The sun has been lost!" In the morning when the

sun rises, the child will rejoice at its return. A child doesn't know the truth behind the rising and setting of the sun. My children, it is for the same reason that we rejoice and grieve with each loss and gain.

245. Now and then you will see a person herding ducks through the backwaters in a tiny boat. The boat will be so small that the man can't even stand in it comfortably. If he puts his foot in the wrong place, the boat could sink. If he as much as breathes carelessly, the boat will tip—it is that tiny. He guides the ducks and stops them from straying by standing in the boat, slapping the water with his oar. Using his feet, he will scoop out any water that enters the boat. He will also converse with people standing along the shore. From time to time he may smoke. Even though he does all these things in that tiny boat, his mind is always on the oar. If his attention wavers even for a moment, the boat could capsize and he would fall. My children, we should live in this world in a similar way. Whatever work we are doing, our minds should be cantered on God.

246. The folk dancer who dances with a pot on his head performs many different tricks. He dances and rolls on the ground. But his mind is always focused on the pot. Similarly, with practice it becomes possible to fix the mind on God while doing any type of work.

247. Pray to God by crying in solitude. If there is a wound on your body, your mind will always be on that wound. Similarly, we are suffering from the disease of transmigration [birth, death and rebirth]. We should earnestly desire to be cured of this disease. Only then will our prayers be sincere—will our hearts melt with love for God.

248. Brahma, Vishnu and Shiva[3] create, nourish and destroy desires. Humans create and nourish their desires, but they do not destroy their desires. My

---

[3] Brahma, Vishnu and Shiva are the three aspects of God associated with the creation, preservation and the dissolution of the universe.

children, what is needed today is the destruction of desires.

249. Those who work in an office or bank handle millions of rupees, but they know that the money doesn't belong to them. So, they think nothing about it. They also know that their clients are not their family, and that there is no sincerity in the loving attention they are shown by those clients, that it is selfishly motivated. It therefore makes no difference to them if their clients talk to them or not. We should also live like this. If we live with the understanding that nothing and no one in the world is our own, all our troubles will be over.

250. My children, with awareness of the goal comes concentration. It is only through concentration that we will progress.

251. A mango seed is bitter; but if it is cooked properly, many different dishes can be made from it. This requires effort. The *Srimad Bhagavatam* is for seekers.

If read with proper attention, all the principles of spirituality can be found in it. But for those who don't have an inquiring mind, it is only a story. Generally, it isn't good to read the *Bhagavatam* aloud for the sake of making money. But if a householder cannot make ends meet, then it isn't wrong for him or her to read this book as a way of earning money.

252. If you want to live comfortably in a place that is full of decaying garbage, you have to remove the garbage and burn it. Only then can you live there. Could you do japa and meditate among all that rubbish? The stinking garbage would make you restless. *Homas* [worship ceremony using sacrificial fires] and *yagnas* [offerings] are conducted in order to purify the atmosphere. It is because of this that we get pure air. But God does not require *homas* and *yagnas*.

253. In the name of politics, people don't hesitate to commit murders or spend huge amounts of money. Millions of rupees have been spent for a handful of rocks from the moon. But people are rarely interested

in doing *homas* and *yagnas*, which cost a great deal less and are highly beneficial for society. If these holy sacrifices are not done, that can be accepted, but to condemn them without understanding their benefits is ludicrous. This is blindness.

254. My children, you can live a spiritual life and a worldly life at the same time. But no matter what sort of life you live, it should be possible for you to perform your actions without any attachments or expectations.

Suffering results from thinking, "I am doing this, therefore I must get its reward." Also, we should never think that our wife, husband or child is ours. If we have the attitude that everything belongs to God, there will be no attachment. When we die, our husband, wife and children will not come with us. Only God is eternal.

255. However much wealth we have, unless its value and the way it should be used are properly understood, only suffering will result. My children,

even if you have abundant wealth, the pleasure you derive from it is only temporary; it cannot give you eternal happiness. Didn't kings like Kamsa and Hiranyakashipu possess huge wealth? In spite of possessing everything, what peace of mind did Ravana have? They all strayed from the path of Truth and lived arrogantly. They did so many prohibited things. What was the result of that? They lost all peace and quietude of mind.

256. Amma isn't saying that people should discard their wealth. If we understand how to use our wealth in the proper way, peace and happiness will become our wealth. My children, for those who are fully devoted to God, material wealth is like cooked rice into which sand has fallen.

Freedom from Suffering

257. The fruit of any action can be countered by another action. If a stone is thrown upwards, we can catch it before it falls to the ground. Likewise, the result of any action can be changed in its course. There is no need to grieve and brood over your fate. Your fate can be altered by God's resolve. A person's horoscope may show a strong probability of marriage, but if he or she does spiritual practice from a young age, this prospect may change. There are examples of this even in the epics.

258. A person who is travelling down a river doesn't bother with thinking about the river's origin. In the past, we may have made many mistakes. It is of no use thinking or worrying about such thi ngs. Strive to shape the future. This is what is needed.

259. My children, never think, "I am a sinner. I am not capable of anything." No matter how decayed a colocasia root may be, if there is even a tiny portion

of that root that hasn't decayed, a sprout will grow from it. Likewise, even if there is only a trace of a spiritual *samskara* [disposition] in us, we can progress by holding onto it.

260. All along we have been thinking that the body is of supreme and lasting importance. This has caused us a lot of suffering. Now let us think in the opposite way. The Self is eternal, and it is the Self that is to be realized. If that thought becomes firmly fixed in our minds, our suffering will be eliminated and there will be only bliss.

261. If you are carrying a heavy load, the mere thought that a resting place is nearby will make you feel at ease, for soon you will be able to unburden yourself of your load. On the other hand, if you think that the resting place is far away, the weight will seem heavier. Similarly, when we think that God is close to us, all our burdens are lessened.

Once you have stepped onto a boat or a bus, why would you continue to carry your luggage? Put it down! Likewise, dedicate everything to God. He will protect you.

262. Wherever people go, they find fault with those places. Their minds become restless because of this. So this habit should be changed. We should forget about the shortcomings of the place we are in and try to discover what is useful there and respect it. This is what is needed. Always see only the good everywhere and in everything; then all your suffering will come to an end.

263. Suppose we fall into a hole. Do we poke our own eyes because they didn't guide us properly? Just as we endure any defects in our own eyesight, we should be compassionate towards others, always putting up with their shortcomings.

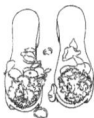

Vasanas

Innate Tendencies

264. Even if there is just one ant in the sugar, the ant should be removed. Otherwise, if it remains, more ants will follow. Similarly, even a small trace of selfishness will pave the way for other vasanas to follow.

265. To exhaust the *vasanas* and destroy the mind (ego) are the same thing. That itself is liberation.

266. The first *vasana* in an individual soul is derived from God, and karma begins from this. It is due to karma that a new birth takes place. The wheel of birth, death and rebirth goes on revolving like this. Only through the exhaustion of one's vasanas is it possible to escape from this. Spiritual activities such as *satsang*, devotional singing and meditation are helpful in exhausting one's *vasanas*.

267. A person's *vasanas* will remain until he or she

has attained liberation. Only in the state of liberation will the vasanas be completely eliminated. Until that state is reached the spiritual aspirant should proceed with utmost discrimination, for until then his or her downfall is possible at any moment. Those who drive on busy roads have to be very careful. If their eyes are diverted even for a moment, an accident could occur. While driving on open ground, there is nothing to fear because only the driver and the car are there. In the beginning of spiritual life, everything is dangerous; utmost care and alertness should be exercised. In the state of liberation, there is only the pure Self—there is no duality and thus no danger.

268. The *vasanas* of a liberated soul are not *vasanas* in the real sense. Their anger, for example, is only an external show. They are absolutely pure within. Quicklime may appear to have the form of a shell, but if you touch it, it will crumble.

269. My children, only a spiritual master can completely remove your *vasanas*. Otherwise one has to

have been born with a powerful spiritual disposition. The jackal will think, "I will never again howl when I see a dog!" but the moment it sees a dog it will be the same old story. It is the same with the *vasanas*.

270. It is not easy to eliminate the flow of thoughts; this is an advanced state. You can destroy impure thoughts by increasing pure thoughts.

271. The negative *vasanas* are not going anywhere. But it is possible to eliminate them with good thoughts, just as when we have salt water in a container and keep adding pure water to it—the salt water will gradually lose its saltiness.

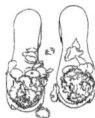

Siddhis

Psychic Powers

272. My children, the display of *siddhis* beyond a certain limit goes against nature. When *siddhis* are shown, people feel attracted to them. Realized souls will, as far as possible, avoid showing their psychic powers. And even if they do, they do not lose anything by it. If the power involved in accomplishing a psychic phenomenon is used to change a person into a *sannyasi*, that will benefit the world. If a seeker becomes fascinated with *siddhis*, he or she will swerve from the goal.

273. Realized souls do not display their powers. If they show them at all, it is very unusual. Due to particular circumstances their powers may arise spontaneously, but they are not meant to entertain onlookers. Don't strive to attain *siddhis*. They are impermanent. A divine incarnation comes to remove desires, not to create them.

Samadhi

274. My children, *sahaja samadhi* [natural abidance in the Self] is perfection. The soul that realizes this state sees the divine principle in everything. Such a soul perceives only pure consciousness everywhere, free from any taint of *maya* [illusion]. Just as a sculptor looks at a stone and sees only the image that can be chiselled out of it, a *mahatma* sees only the all-pervading Divinity in everything.

275. Imagine that there is a rubber ball and a ring within each of us. The ball, which is the mind, is always bouncing up and down, and the ring is our goal. Sometimes the ball will get caught in the ring and stop moving. This can be called *samadhi*. But the ball doesn't rest there permanently; it will begin to move up and down again. Eventually, a state will be reached in which the ball rests permanently in the ring and there is no further motion. This state is called *sahaja samadhi*.

276. By meditating on a form, *savikalpa samadhi* [perceiving ultimate Reality while retaining a sense of duality] can be attained. When one sees the form of one's Beloved Deity, the attitude of 'I' is there; thus there is duality. In formless meditation, since there is no trace of a sense of 'I', the attitude of duality has been completely destroyed. *Nirvikalpa samadhi* is attained in this way.

277. In the state of *nirvikalpa samadhi*, there is no entity to say "I am Brahman." One has merged with That. When an ordinary person attains *nirvikalpa samadhi*, he or she cannot return. At the time of getting absorbed in *samadhi*, since the soul has made no resolve (to return), he or she will leave the body right away. When a soda bottle is opened, the gas is released with a loud pop, merging with the air outside. In this way the soul merges with Brahman forever. Only the divine incarnations can sustain their bodies after entering *nirvikalpa samadhi*. Being aware of the purpose of their incarnation and maintaining

their resolve, they descend into the world again and again.

278. My children, for a divine incarnation there are no such distinctions as *nirvikalpa samadhi* or the states above and below that. The divine incarnations have only a few limitations which they themselves have assumed in order to accomplish the purpose for which they have been born.

279. Even after experiencing *nirvikalpa samadhi*, everyone will not be equal. There is a difference between a spiritual aspirant who has experienced the state of *samadhi* and a divine incarnation. The difference can be compared to that of a person who has just visited Bombay and has returned, and someone who lives there permanently. If they are asked whether they have ever been to Bombay, both will say yes, but the one who lives in Bombay will have a thorough knowledge of the place.

280. Do you know what the state of *samadhi* is like?

There is only bliss. No happiness or sorrow. There is no 'I' or 'you.' This state can be compared to deep sleep, but there is a difference: in *samadhi* there is complete awareness, while in sleep there is no awareness. There is no 'I' or 'you' or 'us' during sleep; it is only when we wake up that 'I', 'you', and the world emerge, and in our ignorance we give them reality.

281. It isn't possible to describe the experience of Brahmanhood. It is a purely subjective experience. Even worldly experiences can be difficult to put into words. Suppose you have a headache. Would you be able to explain exactly how much pain you feel? If that isn't possible, how could it be possible to express in words the experience of Brahman? It cannot be done.

Creation

282. My children, due to the primordial resolve, a vibration arose in Brahman. From that vibration came the three *gunas*: *sattva* [goodness, purity, serenity], *rajas* [activity, passion] and tamas [darkness, inertia, ignorance]. The three *gunas* are represented by the Trinity of Brahma, Vishnu and Shiva. They are all within ourselves. All that is seen to exist in the universe exists within ourselves.

283. On the relative plane, the Self is both the individual soul and the supreme Self. The individual soul is the enjoyer of the fruit of his or her *karma* [actions]. The supreme Self is the witnessing consciousness. It does not do anything; it is inactive.

284. Only when *maya* [illusion] exists is there a God. When we transcend *maya* by constant spiritual practice, we attain the state of Brahman. In that state, not even a trace of *maya* exists.

285. My children, *mithya* does not mean non-existent; it means ever-changing. For example, first there are beans, then there is the dish made of beans with spices, fried in oil [*vada* patties]. The form has changed, but the substance does not disappear.

286. Even if the seashore is dirty, we still enjoy the beauty of the sea, don't we? The mind doesn't dwell on the litter. Similarly, when the mind is fixed on God, it doesn't get ensnared in *maya*.

287. You may consider a needle insignificant because it is cheap. However, the value of something isn't determined by its cost, but by its use. To Amma, a needle is not insignificant. Whatever the object may be, its usefulness and not its price is what should be considered. If we see things in this way, then nothing is insignificant.

288. There is a group of people who contend that creation has never taken place. In sleep we do not know anything. At that time, there is no today or

tomorrow, there is no one—no I, you, husband, wife, child or body. This is an example to show that Brahman still exists as nothing but Brahman. The notion of 'I' and 'my' is the cause of all troubles. One may ask, "Is there not an entity that enjoys the sleep and having woken up says, 'I slept well'?" We say we slept well only because of the satisfaction and well-being the body derived from the sleep.

Rationalism

289. My children, because of the quarrels created by a few religious fanatics, where is the logic in saying that temples and places of worship are unnecessary? Would those who state such things also argue that due to the mistakes of a few doctors, we should do away with doctors and hospitals altogether? Of course not. Religious conflicts need to be eliminated, not the temples of God.

290. In the olden days, those who were rationalists still loved people. But what are today's rationalists like? Simply posing as rationalists, they inflate their egos and only trouble others. A true rationalist is someone who is dedicated to the principles of truth; someone who dearly loves others, even at the cost of his or her own life. God will kneel before such a person. But how many people of this kind are there today?

291. When devotion and reverence develop in a

believer, qualities such as love, compassion, truth, righteousness and justice also develop within that person. Others who approach him or her will be given peace and solace. This is the benefit the world derives from a true believer in God. But today's rationalists grab onto two or three words from some book, without having properly studied the scriptures or anything else, and they create a hue and a cry. This is why Amma says that the rationalism of today will only pave the way for downfall.

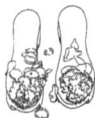

Nature

292. The actions of humanity condition the grace of Nature.

293. My children, Nature is a book to be studied. Each object in nature is a page of that book.

294. Spiritual aspirants utilize the energy of nature for their meditation, nourishment and many other purposes. At least ten percent of the energy and resources we take from Nature should be used for the sake of helping other people. Life is useless otherwise.

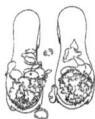

Children, also remember

295. We shouldn't get angry at a person who is unrighteous. If anger arises, it would be towards the person's actions, and not towards him or her.

296. My children, eat to live; sleep to awaken.

297. My children, the goal of life is Self-realization. Strive for that. If there is a wound, we will apply medicine to it only after washing away all the dirt and thus cleaning the wound. Otherwise, the wound will get infected and won't heal. In the same way, the ego should be washed away with devotion, and knowledge should be applied. Only then will we become expansive.

298. We came from God. A faint awareness of this is present in us. This awareness should become full and complete.

299. Out of dirty compost plants emerge bearing beautiful, fragrant flowers. In the same way, drawing

strength from the trials and tribulations of life, grow into greatness.

300. All around us, there are countless people struggling without a house, clothes, food or medical care. With the money one person spends in a year on cigarettes, a small cottage could be built for a homeless person. When we develop compassion for the poor, our selfishness will disappear. We are not giving up anything then; on the contrary, we will derive satisfaction from the happiness of others. When we are free of selfishness, we become fit for God's grace.

301. My children, only those who have studied can teach. Only those who have can give. And only those who are completely free from sorrow can completely free others from sorrow.

302. Every place has a heart centre. It is there that all the energy will be concentrated. In the same way, India is the heart of the world. *Sanatana Dharma* [the eternal religion], which originated here in India, is

the source of all other paths. When the very word 'Bharatam' [India] is heard, we experience the pulse of peace, beauty and light. The reason is that India is the land of the *mahatmas*. It is the *mahatmas* who transmit the life force not only to India, but to the whole world.

303. God-consciousness permeates the coolness of a breeze, the vastness of the sky, the beauty of the full moon, all beings and all things. To realize this is the goal of human life. In this Kali Yuga, a group of young people, sacrificing everything, will go around spreading spiritual glory everywhere.

304. My children, look up at the sky. Be like the sky—vast, peaceful and all-encompassing

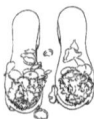

Glossary

Avatar: 'Descent.' An incarnation of the Divine. The aim of a God-incarnation is to protect the good, destroy evil, restore righteousness in the world, and lead humanity to the spiritual goal of Self-realization. It is very rare for an incarnation to be a full descent (*purnavatar*).

Bhajan: Devotional song.

Brahmacharya: 'Abidance in Brahman.' Celibacy and discipline of the mind and the senses.

Brahma Sutras: Aphorisms by Sage Badarayana (Veda Vyasa) that expound Vedantic philosophy.

Bhakti: Devotion

Bhakti yoga: 'Union through *bhakti*.' The path of devotion and love. The way of attaining Self-realization through devotion and complete surrender to God.

Dharma: 'That which upholds the universe.' *Dharma* has many meanings, including the divine law, the law of existence in accordance with divine harmony, righteousness, religion, duty, responsibility, virtue, justice, goodness and truth. *Dharma* signifies the inner principles of religion. The ultimate *dharma* of a human being is to realize his or her own innate Divinity.

Diksha: Initiation.

Guna: Primal Nature [*prakriti*] consists of three *gunas*, i.e., fundamental qualities or tendencies, which underlie all manifestation: *sattva*, *rajas*, and *tamas*. These three *gunas* continually act and react with each other. The phenomenal world is composed of different combinations of the three *gunas*.

Guru: 'One who removes the darkness of ignorance.' Spiritual master/guide.

Japa: The repetition of a mantra.

Jnana yoga: 'Union through *jnana*.' The path of Knowledge. Knowledge of the Self and of the true nature of the world. Involves a deep, sincere study of the holy scriptures, detachment (*vaira-*

gya), discrimination (*viveka*), meditation and the intellectual method of self-inquiry ("Who/What am 'I'?") and ("I am Brahman"), which is used to break through the illusion of maya and attain God-Realization.

Karma yoga: 'Union through action.' The spiritual path of detached, selfless service and of dedicating the fruit of all one's actions to God.

Krishna: 'He who draws us to himself', 'the Dark One.' The principal incarnation of Vishnu, God in His/Her aspect as the Preserver. He was born into a royal family, but grew up with foster parents and lived as a young cowherd in Vrindavan, where he was loved and worshipped by his devoted companions, the gopis [cowherd girls and milkmaids] and gopas [cowherd boys]. Krishna later became the ruler of Dwaraka. He was a friend of and adviser to his cousins, the Pandavas, especially Arjuna, to whom he revealed his teachings in the *Bhagavad Gita*.

Mahatma: 'Great soul.' When Mother uses the word '*mahatma*', She is referring to a Self-realized being.

Mala: Rosary, usually made of rudraksha seeds, tulasi wood or sandalwood beads.

Mantra: Sacred formula or prayer. Through constant repetition, it awakens the seeker's dormant spiritual powers and helps him or her to reach the goal. It is most effective if received from a true spiritual master.

Narasimha: The divine man-lion. Partial incarnation of Vishnu.

Ojas: Sexual energy transmuted into subtle vital energy through the spiritual practice of a celibate.

Pranayama: Controlling the mind through breath control.

Rishi: *Rsi* = to know. Self-realized seer. Usually refers to the seven *rishis* of ancient India, i.e. Self-realized souls who could 'see' the Supreme Truth and expressed this insight through the composition of the Vedas.

Samadhi: *Sam* = with; *adhi* = the Lord. Oneness with God. A state of deep, one-pointed concentration, in which all thoughts subside, the mind enters into a state of complete stillness in which only Pure Consciousness remains, as one abides in the *Atman* (Self).

Samskara: *Samskara* has two meanings: The totality of impressions imprinted in the mind by experiences (from this or earlier lives), which influence the life of a human being—his or her nature, actions, state of mind, etc. The kindling of the right understanding (knowledge) within each person, leading to the refinement of his or her character.

Sannyasi or sannyasini: A monk or nun who has taken formal vows of renunciation. A *sannyasi(ni)* traditionally wears an ochre collared cloth representing the burning away of all attachments.

Satguru: A Self-realized spiritual master.

Satsang: *Sat* = truth, being; *sanga* = association with. Being in the company of the holy, wise and virtuous. Also a spiritual discourse by a sage or scholar.

Srimad Bhagavatam: One of eighteen scriptures known as the *Puranas*, which describes the incarnations of Lord Vishnu, especially, and in great detail, the life of Sri Krishna, including his childhood. It places great emphasis on the path of devotion.

Tamas: Darkness, inertia, apathy, ignorance. Tamas is one of the three gunas or fundamental qualities of Nature.

Tapas: 'Heat.' Self-discipline, austerities, penance and self-sacrifice; spiritual practices which burn up the impurities of the mind.

Vasana: *Vas* = living, remaining. *Vasanas* are the latent tendencies or subtle desires within the mind which have a tendency to manifest into action and habits. *Vasanas* are the collected results of the impressions of experiences [*samskaras*] which exist in the subconscious.

Yoga: 'To unite.' A set of methods through which one can attain oneness with the Divine. A Path which leads to Self-realization.

Yogi: Someone who is established in the practice of *yoga*, or is established in union with the Supreme Spirit.

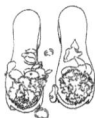

Book Catalog
By Author

Sri Mata Amritanandamayi Devi
108 Quotes On Faith
108 Quotes On Love
Compassion, The Only Way To Peace:
   Paris Speech
Cultivating Strength And Vitality
Living In Harmony
May Peace And Happiness Prevail:
   Barcelona Speech
May Your Hearts Blossom:
   Chicago Speech
Practice Spiritual Values And Save The
   World: Delhi Speech
The Awakening Of Universal
   Motherhood: Geneva Speech
The Eternal Truth
The Infinite Potential Of Women:
   Jaipur Speech
Understanding And Collaboration
   Between Religions
Unity Is Peace: Interfaith Speech

Swami Amritaswarupananda Puri
Ammachi: A Biography
Awaken Children, Volumes 1-9
From Amma's Heart
Mother Of Sweet Bliss
The Color Of Rainbow

Swami Jnanamritananda Puri
Eternal Wisdom, Volumes 1-2

Swami Paramatmananda Puri
On The Road To Freedom Volumes 1-2
Talks, Volumes 1-6

Swami Purnamritananda Puri
Unforgettable Memories

Swami Ramakrishnananda Puri
Eye Of Wisdom
Racing Along The Razor's Edge
Secret Of Inner Peace
The Blessed Life
The Timeless Path
Ultimate Success

Swamini Krishnamrita Prana
Love Is The Answer
Sacred Journey
The Fragrance Of Pure Love
Torrential Love

M.A. Center Publications
1,000 Names Commentary
Archana Book (Large)
Archana Book (Small)
Being With Amma
Bhagavad Gita
Bhajanamritam, Volumes 1-6
Embracing The World
For My Children
Immortal Light
Lead Us To Purity
Lead Us To The Light
Man And Nature
My First Darshan
Puja: The Process Of Ritualistic
   Worship
Sri Lalitha Trishati Stotram

Amma's Websites

AMRITAPURI—Amma's Home Page
Teachings, Activities, Ashram Life, eServices, Yatra, Blogs and News
http://www.amritapuri.org

AMMA (Mata Amritanandamayi)
About Amma, Meeting Amma, Global Charities, Groups and Activities and Teachings
http://www.amma.org

EMBRACING THE WORLD®
Basic Needs, Emergencies, Environment, Research and News
http://www.embracingtheworld.org

AMRITA UNIVERSITY
About, Admissions, Campuses, Academics, Research, Global and News
http://www.amrita.edu

THE AMMA SHOP—Embracing the World® Books & Gifts Shop
Blog, Books, Complete Body, Home & Gifts, Jewelry, Music and Worship
http://www.theammashop.org

IAM—Integrated Amrita Meditation Technique®
Meditation Taught Free of Charge to the Public, Students, Prisoners and Military
http://www.amma.org/groups/north-america/projects/iam-meditation-classes

AMRITA PUJA
Types and Benefits of Pujas, Brahmasthanam Temple, Astrology Readings, Ordering Pujas
http://www.amritapuja.org

GREENFRIENDS
Growing Plants, Building Sustainable Environments, Education and Community Building
http://www.amma.org/groups/north-america/projects/green-friends

FACEBOOK
This is the Official Facebook Page to Connect with Amma
https://www.facebook.com/MataAmritanandamayi

DONATION PAGE
Please Help Support Amma's Charities Here:
http://www.amma.org/donations